HOUSING

Did it have to be like this?

*A socialist critique of
New Labour's performance*

In 1997, most Labour-controlled local authorities hoped an incoming Labour Government with a massive majority would reverse some of the worst excesses of Margaret Thatcher and John Major. They hoped for a new settlement between central and local government and a future in which they would be able to invest again in long-overdue maintenance and modernisation of council stock. They hoped to be able to build again; responding to the many thousands waiting for council housing by this time.

Instead, they have faced a government which has determinedly continued to asset-strip the public sector. They have been faced with Hobson's Choice in relation to maintenance and modernisation: that is, variations of privatisation. New council building on the scale required to tackle the housing crisis has become a dim memory for those 1990s Housing Committee members. And what of council housing itself? Transformed into '*social housing*,' apparently overrun by '*anti-social behaviour*' and with tenants whose vulnerabilities are such that they need to be '*mixed*' (that is, lost) in owner-occupied estates.

This pamphlet will identify the best of what was achieved by Labour governments in the past, by Labour ministers struggling against considerable opposition to achieve progressive legislation and large building programmes. This will be compared with what New Labour, with a massive electoral majority, has achieved in relation to council housebuilding and maintenance, anti-social behaviour and creating mixed communities. What have been the effects of the twin restrictions on local authorities – in relation to new building and funding to achieve the Decent Homes Standard? Should council or housing association landlords have substantial powers over tenants' personal behaviour, and has New Labour emphasis on dealing with anti-social behaviour changed the way that *social housing* is regarded? Finally, we will explore the different ways in which New Labour has used the idea of creating '*mixed communities*' for council (and housing association) rented housing and consider whether it was realistic or whether the idea was deployed as a political smokescreen, designed to hide the reality of declining council and housing association house-building for rent and the growing difficulties for all low-income residents in dealing with the vagaries of an increasingly flexible labour market.

Back to the future

Looking back over the history of social housing in England and Wales, Michael Harloe identified two different *'conditions'* or *'states'* for council housing, *'mass'* provision and *'residual'* provision. He argued that 'mass provision'

> '... gains major significance and state support only in "abnormal" times, that is, when varying combinations of social, economic and political circumstances limit the scope for private provision **and** when this limitation is of strategic significance for certain aspects of the maintenance and development of the capitalist social and economic system.'
>
> (Harloe, 1995, p7)

He identified different *'social structures of accumulation'* over the period of the twentieth century to help him analyse why council housing had advanced and retreated over this time. The first was liberal capitalism surviving up to the Second World War. The second was welfare capitalism developing up to the early 1970s. The third stage, unnamed by him, was marked by continuous capitalist restructuring and the growth of the flexible labour market. He argued that to begin to explain why council housing developed as *'mass'* provision at specific times, the economic, social and political context in which particular governments worked was of key importance. In addition, there was also the question of whether particular governments had the organisational means when they were in power to provide *mass* rented housing. So understanding what happened was broader than considering measurable housing needs and looking at political parties' formal manifestos, specific housing policies and the predilections, competence and influence of the politicians involved.

It is possible to identify two such moments – a short period in the 1920s during which John Wheatley's legislation enabled local authorities to build large numbers of good quality council houses for the first time, and the period immediately after the Second World War in which Aneurin Bevan as Minister of Health did similarly. We will provide a brief outline of these achievements first and then, against this background, argue that New Labour in 1997 was faced with a similar *'strategic'* moment but one based on a growing flexible labour market and a very recent history of difficulties with owner-occupation. How will New Labour's achievements be viewed against the best in socialist housing history?

How did Wheatley and Bevan do it?

John Wheatley's legacy

John Wheatley was a Clydeside industrialist who had been an influential figure in the Glasgow rent strike. His determination to secure better housing for working class people derived from this experience (Hannan, 1988). He was leader of the Independent Labour Party (ILP) group of MPs in the Parliamentary Labour Party which formed a minority Labour Government in 1924 (lasting for a year, before the Liberals withdrew their support, forcing another election following which the Conservatives returned to power). Against a background of minority government and determination by the Prime Minster and most of the Cabinet to 'dispel any apprehension as to the Government's radicalism' (Miliband, 1979, p108) he achieved the enactment of the Housing (Financial Provisions) Act 1924, better known as the Wheatley Act. This led to the first long-term programme of good-standard council housing produced in this country. As Pelling (1972, p57) remarked,

> *'It was an interesting fact that the one minister to distinguish himself as the master of the difficult act of securing social legislation in a minority government, was the one representative of the new ILP Left in the Cabinet.'*

Given the Government's precarious position, it was clear that a more extensive socialist strategy could not be achieved, involving land nationalization, firmer control of the building industry and alternatives to private funding for local authority building. Despite this, Wheatley's so-called Gentleman's Agreement, (see Merrett, 1979, pp45-6) secured to ensure co-operation between the building unions and employers in the construction industry, formed the basis of the expanding programme. The Agreement was unprecedented and the targets for local authority building were enormous. To build the programme's momentum, housebuilding (using the Wheatley subsidy or earlier less generous arrangements) would be measured every two years against targets. If they were achieved, the programme and subsidies to local authorities continued. Subsidies would be withdrawn if they had not built a minimum of two-thirds of the target for the two year period preceding 1927, 1930, 1933 and 1936. The targets set are in Table 1 below and were intended to encourage forward planning.

Table 1: Housebuilding targets for local authorities

1925-6	1928-9	1931-2	1934-5
95,000	128,000	180,000	225,000

Source: Merrett, 1979, p46

These can be compared with the reported numbers built. Just concentrating on local authority housebuilding completions, Merrett (1979, p320) has indicated that the figures were 73,370 (1925 and 1926), 190,169 (1928 and 1929), 143,009 (1931 and 1932) and 129,669 (1934 and 1935). The breakdown of building figures attributable to the two most important but different subsidies (Wheatley and Chamberlain) can be seen in Table 2.

Table 2 : Local authority dwellings built in England and Wales in 1924-35 under the 1923 and 1924 Housing Acts * (in thousands)

Year ending 31 March	1924	1925	1926	1927	1928	1929	1930	1931	1932	1933	1934	1935	Total
1923 Act	3.8	15.3	16.2	14.1	13.8	5.1	5.6	–	–	1.4a	–	–	75.3
1924 Act	–	2.5	26.9	59.1	90.1	50.6	54.6	52.5	65.2	47.1	44.8	11.1	504.5
Total	3.8	17.8	43.1	73.2	103.9	55.7	60.2	52.2	65.2	48.5	44.8	11.1	579.8

a = *Transferred from the 1924 Act*

1923 Act = Housing Act 1923, often referred to as the Chamberlain Act. This was preferred by Conservative and Liberal local authorities as its objective was to encourage the private sector to build small houses for sale as well as rent. The subsidy was lower than that in the Wheatley legislation and there was no expected local rates contribution.

1924 Act = Housing Act, 1924, often referred to as the Wheatley Act. This was preferred by Labour local authorities as there was an increased subsidy and extended period over which it was payable. It allowed local contributions from the rates. Better housebuilding standards were possible and the emphasis was on local authority building.

Source: Bowley, 1945, p271 from which this table was created by Merrett, 1979, p47

The variability in local authority output during these years (which can be seen in Merrett's figures and Table 2) is partly explained by the deteriorating economic situation developing during the 1920s and 1930s. The building rate in individual local authorities also depended on the political party in power locally, the degree to which the private sector was building in that area and the financial situation of the local authority (see Daunton, 1984, p20 for more detailed discussion). For example, the first Labour council in Sheffield, elected in 1926, immediately and dramatically increased the housebuilding programme to a minimum of 1000 houses a year (peaking at 2500 in one year). The newly established public works department built 7844 council houses in the period 1926 to 1932 financed with Wheatley subsidies. The council preferred this to employing the private builders used by previous administrations which had proved expensive because poor initial workmanship created large repair bills (Rowlinson, 1932).

Wheatley's more generous subsidy was intended to enable local authorities to charge rents that could be paid by working class people and was widely used across the country especially by Labour authorities. They saw the subsidy as one way in which they could improve working class living conditions on a dramatic scale. Nevertheless, rents were too high for those families where the main wage earner had a very low or erratic income or was unemployed (see Burnett, p238-40 for a detailed discussion). Most new council tenants living in Wheatley's estates of parlour/non-parlour houses were better off working class households. In the 1920s, in addition to the rent there often were other unavoidable costs. The effective suburbanization of former inner-city residents meant that for many wage earners (who were usually men) there were increased costs in getting to work. Although there were exceptions, many new housing estates also had few if any community facilities. For women and children, simply travelling to visit shops or to see relatives was another new pressure on the family budget.

From the council landlord's point of view, in this early period of *'mass'* council housing, housing management became increasingly de-personalised and semi-professionalised. Although some tenants found it hard to settle in these new houses, (turnover was often high), anti-social behaviour (or nuisance as it was called then) was not a particular problem. Local authority staff (often from different departments) managed individual areas, concentrating on the elements of *estate management* (allocations, rents and repairs). Local authorities opted for this rather than the form of housing management promoted by Octavia Hill with its intrusive, *overt* social control. As Daunton (1984, p25) dryly remarked,

> '... tenants were informed of the social behaviour which was required of them by the Council through the issue of handbooks, the exclusion of publicans, and the encouragement of gardening.'

Aneurin Bevan's legacy

Fast forward twenty years. In 1945, a majority Labour Government was in power for the first time following the Second World War and Aneurin Bevan was Minister of Health. *Let Us Face the Future*, the Party's election manifesto, had promised to start housebuilding *'with the maximum practical speed.'* The task of reconstruction following the War was enormous: the Ministry thought that 750,000 houses needed to be built in five years but that turned out to be a gross underestimate. Bevan turned to local authorities. Most new building was to be completed by them and it was to be available for rent not sale. Subsidies were increased to enable local authorities to build to good standards. He believed (against continuing Conservative criticism in the House) that only local authorities could effectively and fairly plan to provide the housing needed by families who were homeless or living in bomb-damaged accommodation. Consequently, only 20% of the total new building planned was reserved for the private builder to build for sale *and* they had to secure a development licence from the local authority before building started. In Bevan's view, private sector builders could not be used to build on the scale or to the standards required. Their search for profit pre-empted that.

> '... if we are to have any correspondence between the size of the building force on the sites and the actual provision of the material coming forward to the sites from the industries, there must be some planning. If we are to plan we have to plan with plannable instruments, and the speculative builder, by his very nature, is not a plannable instrument.'

(quoted in Foot, 1997, p269)

In addition to this, he '... *never allowed anyone working in his department to relapse into the delusion that building houses was solely a question of economics or business. People had to live in them*' (Foot, 1997, p274). He insisted on adopting Dudley Committee space standards (often increased by individual local authorities) although they were sometimes difficult to maintain in the face of enormous political pressure to build quickly, in large numbers.

The Dudley Committee's improved individual housebuilding standards (especially for space and facilities) went hand in hand with an emphasis from the Ministry of Health's civil servants (through official advice) and from Bevan as Minister (through speeches) on ensuring that people from different classes were able to obtain council housing. His comments about the doctor, grocer and farm labourer living on the same street have often been quoted. What he wanted was for new council tenants to experience what he described as *'the living tapestry of a mixed community'* (quoted in Foot, 1997, p273). In the 1940s, this translated into building estates with different house types and sizes and mixing family with single person and older people's housing. These *mixed developments* with an emphasis on creating neighbourhoods had their origins in American planning from the 1920s (Burnett, 1986, p297) but chimed well with Bevan's insistence that council housing should not be restricted to *'housing for the working classes'* but should be available for anyone who wanted to rent. The irony was, though, that some local authorities had already begun to institutionalize the practice of putting poorer people in poorer houses in their 1930s slum clearance activities. This was to come back and haunt council housing in terms of allocations and general image in future years despite Bevan's desire for something radically different.

Nevertheless, battling against acute shortages of bricks, slates and timber, the figures for new homes gradually increased. In 1946, 55,400 were completed, in 1947, 139,690 and in 1948, 227,616. As Michael Foot points out, if the figures for other forms of major repair and rebuilding work done to ensure people had a roof over their heads had been included the government would not have been very short of the 750,000 figure by 1948 (Foot, 1997, p278). But the numbers declined thereafter as the Government itself reigned in local authorities in the face of worsening economic circumstances. Put simply, the Cabinet decided that the country could not afford council housebuilding of this standard, on this scale, at this time.

Three features emerge from this period worth consideration in current times. The commitment to local authorities is the first notable feature of policy then. Bevan saw that they could be used to build a large programme and they could be subject to plans and targets in a way in which the private sector could not. Harloe has said that this period represents one in which Britain came closest to a socialised housing market (Harloe, 1995, p283). The *'nationalisation of development rights'* with the restrictions on private building for sale was *'revolutionary'* in his view. Others, looking more broadly, might cast some doubt on this analysis (see Miliband, 1972, pp272-298) but local authorities were clearly given a great deal of encouragement to build council housing on a scale not seen since the late 1920s. This approach responded to what the public expected of this majority Labour government, encapsulating attitudes born of war-time experiences about what the state and local authorities should do to improve the lives of people who had survived the devastation and were still being rationed in basic goods.

This leads to two other important aspects from that time, standards and scale. The Dudley Committee standards and the stream of advice which emerged over the years from the Ministry of Health (or its successors) helped create a sector where generally standards were good and higher than the private sector equivalents (Burnett, 1986, p296). New council tenants came from all sections of society, given that bombing had been indiscriminate. They were not a stigmatized minority. The council housing built then was valued for its high quality and standing. It was only later that concerns about tenant behaviour became more noticeable in the sector, usually when considering the areas of poorer quality council housing that had been built with less generous subsidies or with experimental or untried built forms (sometimes specifically linked to rehousing people from housing designated as 'slums').

Finally, scale. Although criticized for not achieving 750,000 new rented homes in five years, Bevan was working in extraordinary times and his achievement as it stands is significant. It is ironic that some housing professionals and academics of today remember his comments about mixed communities while forgetting his commitment to the public sector, to high standards and to a large-scale, planned local authority council housebuilding programme and general rehabilitation works across all housing tenures.

What did New Labour inherit from the Conservatives in 1997?

Fast forward again and we are looking at an incoming Labour government with a massive electoral majority of 197 in 1997. What did they inherit from eighteen years of Conservative government?

The Right to Buy

Firstly, council house sales. The Conservatives had enabled council tenants to purchase their homes with ever increasing discounts. Council house sales peaked in 1989 but were, on their terms, a highly successful privatisation. 1.3 million council houses were sold between 1980 and 1997: an average of 77,500 a year for 17 years (as can be seen in Tables 3a and 3b).

Table 3a: Right to Buy in England – 1980 to 1989

	1980-1985	1986	1987	1988	1989
Local authorities	512,876	73,767	84,007	128,566	139,722
Housing associations	7,990	2,791	2,046	3,323	3,700

Table 3b : Right to Buy in England – 1990 to 1997

	1990	1991	1992	1993	1994	1995	1996	1997
Local authorities	92,995	51,414	41,445	41,188	44,999	33,960	31,781	39,875
Housing associations	3,369	1,871	669	666	831	592	2,380	4,500

Source: Drawn from Table 20a in Wilcox, (2008), p105 using *Housing Statistics*

The Conservatives initially prevented local authorities from using Right to Buy capital receipts except to pay off debt or reduce loan charges attributable to their Housing Revenue Account. This changed from 1981/2, when they were allowed to use a proportion of housing capital receipts (from that year and from their accumulated totals) in their other capital spending. These could be carried forward if a local authority chose. This resulted in a situation in which many authorities, especially in the south (where most sales were), were financing capital expenditure largely from accumulated receipts rather than Housing Investment Programmes (HIPs). The government reacted to this potential loss of control by changing the rules and introducing moratoria, generally creating,

> '... a climate of uncertainty which in some circumstances led to wastage or hurried decisions on major projects, to the winding down of programmes, staff redundancies and other problems.'   Malpass and Murie, 1990, pp106-7

Using receipts to help finance capital spending in this way recycled money, gave a considerable element of control to the centre and reduced the need for central government to make additional expenditure commitments. The way in which the Conservative Government dealt with sales immediately after the 1980 Housing Act was also designed to stamp its authority over local government (see the discussion in Forrest and Murie, 1991, pp200-217). The Labour Party at first opposed the Right to Buy but then supported it because of its popularity with council tenants. This policy was not likely to be changed when New Labour took office although Labour authorities and many housing organisations hoped and expected that there might be significant reductions in discounts and exemptions from the policy in high demand areas of the country, given growing waiting lists and homelessness.

Declining council house building

Under the Conservatives, HIP allocations declined each year because the Government believed that local authorities should not build council houses. Conservative policy placed most local authority landlords (whatever their political hue) in a quandary: repairing and replacing defective housing took up substantial proportions of HIP allocations but how was new council house building to be funded to replace council housing sold and to tackle waiting lists? The results of the Conservative Party's preference for housing associations, (building on a much reduced scale, using combinations of private and gradually-reducing, fixed Housing Association Grant from 1988 onwards), can be seen from Table 4a.

Table 4a : Housing completions in England

	1980	1985	1990	1991	1992	1993	1994	1995	1996	1997
Local authorities	67,337	22,483	13,873	8,051	3,274	1,402	1,094	782	511	290
Housing associations		19,299	11,298	13,821	15,295	20,789	29,779	30,848	30,888	27,025	20,966

Source: Drawn from Table 19b in Wilcox, (2008), p99 using *Housing Statistics*

A relatively small number of local authorities continued to build council housing in the 1980s and early1990s using reserves, local authority Housing Association Grant and their own land, but this was on an ever-reducing scale. Sheffield City Council was one of the few authorities that tried to find another way around increasing central government control and declining HIP allocations. A renewed emphasis on municipal socialism (Blunkett and Green, 1983, p24) meant that senior councillors determined to find ways in which council house repair and modernisation and new building could go hand in hand. By 1986, 20,000 inter-war council homes in Sheffield were awaiting modernisation and *'tens of thousands'* of post-war properties needed *'significant attention'* because of system building failures and other maintenance problems. 3000 had been demolished in the previous three years because of significant system build or wall-tie failure (but could not be replaced within the HIP programme as it stood). Another 2,500 were to be taken out of letting over the next five years for the same reasons. Despite these problems, this authority's HIP allocation had declined from £29,810,000 (in 1978/9) to £22,724,000 in 1985/6 (Wigfield, 1991, p1).

The local authority investigated a number of ways to deal with this situation and decided to work with an association which would build properties on behalf of the council, leasing them back in due course. *'The Partnership'* was established between the City Council and United Kingdom Housing Trust (UKHT) in 1987. UKHT initially raised sufficient finance to build 2000 new homes in the city, designed in close consultation with the council and prospective new tenants. (There was provision for an additional 2000 homes if the initial programme was successful). 60% were for rent and they were leased back to the local authority to manage: council housing in all but ownership (UKHT). This provided replacement rented stock with community facilities in most of the nine sites in which property was built. It also allowed the council's HIP allocation to be used in full for council house repairs and modernisation.

Unsurprisingly, the Conservative Government attempted to stop this development, making it illegal for local authorities to be party to such arrangements (intervening in much the same way as it had done in relation to council house sales). The Minister introduced a specific provision in the Government's Local Government Bill which outlawed lease-back schemes from the following day, in full knowledge of the progress of the Sheffield Partnership scheme (Wigfield, 1991, p20-24 for the full details). However, the Partnership agreement between the City Council and UKHT was signed just 15 minutes before the midnight deadline. But while Sheffield 'succeeded,' most other authorities were not in this position and the problem of growing disrepair and obsolescence remained. This was one area in which local authorities expected more direct investment when New Labour came to power.

Increasing central government control of local authorities

Underlying these issues was a much more significant development: the changing relationship between central and local government. During the 1980s, the Conservative Government gradually increased its powers over local government activity such that by the end of the decade there was very little local autonomy. The first sign of this trend was in 1982 when Norwich City Council was unsuccessful in challenging the Conservative Government's intervention in the way it processed Right to Buy applications. Tightening Government control of council house building, an emphasis on partnerships which often were excessively complicated and overly concerned with 'value for money' (see Jacobs, 1999 for a detailed case study of Hackney) and controls over local expenditure more generally, with the prospect of rate capping, were to follow. But a *'step-change'* (Malpass, 2005, p113) occurred in 1987. The White Paper *Housing: the Government's Proposals* (Department of the Environment, 1987) signalled a new role for local authorities as *'enablers'* not providers of housing for rent. They were expected to transfer their stock to the so-called *'independent rented sector'* (that is private landlords and housing associations) to attain this position. As Malpass pointed out, this represented,

> '... a much more aggressive, in principle challenge to the role that local authorities had developed over a period of seventy years.'   Malpass, 2005, p133

In retrospect, relatively few authorities transferred their stock in the period to 1997. Of those that did, most set up new associations to take over ownership. These were often still seen as connected to the local authority in spirit if not legally – although in the early 1990s, several outgrew their local authority boundaries and, via mergers, extended across the country. There was a geographical pattern to this activity. Most transfers were from rural authorities in the south that had been Liberal and Conservative controlled. Surely this would not continue to be the approach under New Labour?

What has New Labour done?

In its 1997 election manifesto *'New Labour because Britain deserves better'* a supposedly new approach was promised.

> 'In each area of policy a new and distinctive approach has been mapped out, one that differs from the old left and the Conservative right. This is why new Labour is new. New Labour is a party of ideas and ideals but not of outdated ideology. What counts is what works. The objectives are radical. The means will be modern.'

We have already identified that New Labour's election could have been a *strategic moment* for housing (Harloe, 1995). The early 1990s saw a recession, the growth of negative equity and foreclosures on a large scale (Whitehead, Gibb and Stephens, 2005). This made purchase more risky financially. This, combined with the spread of job insecurity associated with the flexible labour market, should have pointed New Labour in the direction of providing a greatly expanded, council housing sector. At the time of New Labour's election victory in 1997, local authorities still managed most housing for rent and could have been used as a vehicle to build on a large scale again. Associations' performance in this regard had been sluggish and they were increasingly reliant on volatile private finance. New Labour had a massive majority and time on its side. It could have easily changed the 'direction of travel' of housing policy but despite the espousal of *'radical'* objectives and *'modern'* means, New Labour chose to maintain many of the main themes and approaches of the Conservatives.

More housing investment?

One immediate problem – for housing at least – was a manifesto pledge to keep within previously agreed Conservative expenditure targets for the first two years. Investment by New Labour for England in each year of its first term of office fell far below what the Conservatives had spent in their last four years: £3.3 billion annually by New Labour over five years to 2003 compared to £4.4 billion by Conservatives in the four years up to 1997 (Wilcox, 2008, Table 57a, p157). This included allowing a redistribution of accumulated right to buy receipts (nearly £5 billion over 1997 to 2002, according to the Green Paper in 2000) most of which was spent by local authorities on repairs and renovation. Typical of many commentators, Norman Perry, former Chief Executive of the Housing Corporation, remarked that in his time (2000 to 2004) the government did *'the minimum necessary'* to deal with housing problems (*Inside Housing*, 2010). Investment later increased (£5 billion for 2001-2004 and £6.8 billion for 2005-2009 – Wilcox, ibid) but what was the money being spent on?

More housebuilding for rent by councils and housing associations?

One direct casualty of this self-inflicted restriction on spending was capital investment to build more housing for rent. At the time, the

Housing: Did it have to be like this?

National Housing Federation (representing associations) and Shelter were both pressing for the need for 100,000 housing association and council rented homes to be built each year to catch up with demand. This did not happen. New building for rent continued to decline: 2003 marked the lowest level since 1935 (see Table 2 to compare figures) and a far cry from the achievements of Wheatley and Bevan. As Malpass (2005, p178) has pointed out,

> 'This is consistent with the known preference of the Blair government for private solutions wherever possible ... but it is interesting that in circumstances where there are clearly acknowledged problems about supply from private enterprise the government has decided not to deploy a means of building houses that had proved very effective in the past. Volume building by local authorities ... is now out of the question. It is a measure of how far the Labour Party has travelled that since 1997 output by social housing providers has continued to fall in both absolute terms and as a proportion of all new building.'

The detail of this depressing and completely avoidable picture can be seen in Table 4b.

Table 4b : Housing completions in England

	1998	1999	2000	2001	2002	2003	2004	2005	2006	2007
Local authorities	243	54	87	160	177	177	131	182	277	345
Housing associations	19,901	17,775	16,681	14,502	13,309	12,882	16,604	17,535	20,752	22,014

Source: Drawn from Table 19b in Wilcox, (2008), p99 using *Housing Statistics*.

A proportion of the association properties were built for sale not rent. It is not possible to distinguish the funding source (for example, what derives from mixed funding including housing association grant/social housing grant , planning gain or building using an association's own resources – see Wilcox, 2009, p14 for further comment).

Associations completed 25, 650 new homes in 2008, the most recent available figures (Wilcox, 2009, p111), but this was due to increased government financial support to avoid a collapse in the housing market. This will not be sustained, given the economic situation.

In retrospect, it is astonishing (and damning) that the right to buy was allowed to continue, even though there was a diminishing supply of new building for rent and it was seriously affecting the supply of council relets. Whilst admitting that *'past policies have starved social housing of investment and* **created ghettoes of deprivation and social exclusion**' (our emphasis), New Labour's approach barely acknowledged new council housebuilding for rent (and provided only for marginal increases in housing association production, too). Instead, it announced in its first Green Paper, *'Quality and choice: a decent home for all'* (DETR, 2000) that it intended to secure a *'decent standard'* for existing social housing by 2010, improvements in management, stock transfer away from local authorities, a more *'coherent'* system of rents and more *'empowerment'* for tenants (p17). Clearly, many council (and housing association) tenants' aspirations to move to a new rented home at some time in the future did not count.

The Right to Buy?

Despite this drastic decline in council housebuilding for rent, the possibility of council (and housing association) purchase remained. Although regarded as the Conservatives' most successful privatisation, it came at a very high cost. New Labour indicated that each of 1.3 million sales had cost the taxpayer £10,000 (DETR, 2000, p36). This adds up to £13 billion over thirty years. Surely New Labour would not continue this?

New Labour's Green Paper (DETR, 2000) admitted that the Right to Buy,

> '... has led to the removal of more desirable homes from the social rented sector, leaving local authorities with a smaller stock of poorer quality properties in which to house people who need their help.'

But from 1998 to 2007, under New Labour nearly 500,000 council homes were sold, an average of 50,000 a year. The detailed pattern of continuing sales, particularly of council stock which was not being replaced, can be seen in Table 5. The figure peaked in 2003 at 85,000 because tenants were trying to avoid reductions in discounts introduced by government regulation in 2002 to restrict sales in high demand areas in the South East and London (Communities and Local Government [CLG] 2007, section 2.4). The most recently available figures for 2008 were 4590 for councils and 1000 for associations and show the impact of the credit crunch on tenants' finances (Wilcox, 2009, p117). As importantly, comparing right-to-buy figures with those for new homes built shows that the *'social rented housing'* has been steadily shrinking through annual stock losses (see Wilcox, 2009, p14).

Housing: Did it have to be like this?

Table 5 : Right to Buy in England – 1998 to 2007

	1998	1999	2000	2001	2002	2003	2004	2005	2006	2007
Local authorities	39,846	51,212	54,856	50,735	58,526	71,404	58,490	29,872	19,350	13,260
Housing associations	4,410	7,250	7,100	8,220	10,470	14,530	8,670	6,360	4,840	3,150

Source: Drawn from Table 20a in Wilcox, (2008), p105 using *Housing Statistics*

Margaret Thatcher had thought that council housing represented *'breeding grounds of socialism, dependency, vandalism and crime'* whereas home ownership inculcated *'all the virtues of good citizenship'* (Gregory, 2009, pp30-1 quoting Campbell, 2003, p234). But what was it that drove New Labour's continuing commitment to the Right to Buy? Sixty-eight percent of the population lived in owner occupied homes at the beginning of the twenty-first century in England. New Labour's Green Paper (DETR, 2000, p30) waxed lyrical about *'sustainable homeownership'* and *'the dream of homeownership,'* an *'aspiration'* it claimed that was shared by *'90%'* of the population. *'Our policies will continue to help people to achieve their aspirations and we expect an increase over the coming years in the number of people who own their own home.'* It included prospective Right to Buy applicants, along with other prospective home owners, in the comment (p37) that it would provide *'further support'* for those,

> *'... on the threshold of homeownership'* and *'... greater help for people on lower incomes to buy their own homes, promoting a culture of opportunity, choice and self-reliance and giving people more of a stake in their housing and neighbourhoods.'*

This ideology of individual ownership and espousal of consumerism (promoted through linking it with ideas such as *'opportunity'*, *'choice'* and *'self-reliance'*) began to be undermined by research: for example, Burrows revealed that a half of all home-owners were living in poverty (Burrows, 2003). Yet New Labour continued to support the extension of home ownership to people who would be considered marginal homeowners at best. Malpass (2008, p12) has noted that owner-occupiers were *'increasingly, and officially, encouraged to see their properties as assets as well as places to live.'* He quoted Yvette Cooper, one former Housing Minister, as explaining in 2005,

> *'... measures to increase access to wealth and homeownership for those on low incomes should be an important part of Labour's third term strategy for social justice.'*

New Labour now saw home ownership as a means by which individuals could take responsibility for their housing, at the same time providing themselves with a means to accumulate 'wealth.' This might be used to pay for services needed later (on retirement) or be inherited by family members. Accumulating this 'wealth' relied on increasing market values, the availability of mortgages and stable, well-paid jobs. Even in benign times, this depends on geography, property type and individual circumstances, but since the 'credit crunch' global financial markets operate like a casino. It is now difficult to predict property values, and surely is a very hazardous way of providing for future service needs. With this in mind, it is difficult to accommodate New Labour's preference for individual home ownership within socialist principles. It is at variance with collective solutions to society's problems which are even more important now that *global* capitalism provides a much riskier financial environment for everyone. Malpass concluded that even if a home was treated simply as an asset, *'housing is unlikely to become a robust and long-term cornerstone of a modernised welfare state ...'* The 'credit crunch' and recession have justified that view.

In the context of owner-occupation becoming increasingly unaffordable and with very little new social rented house building (by councils or housing associations), with lengthening waiting lists and growing homelessness and overcrowding, the continuation of the Right to Buy by New Labour can only be seen as reckless.

Stock transfer

New Labour's election manifesto in 1997 stated that it supported,

> '... *effective schemes to deploy private finance to improve the public housing stock and to introduce greater diversity and choice. Such schemes should only go ahead with the support of the tenants concerned: we oppose the government's threat to hand over council housing to private landlords without the consent of tenants and with no guarantees on rents or security of tenure.'*

In its Green Paper *Quality and Choice* (DETR, 2000) it went on to outline plans for an annual programme of transfers of council housing to newly-designated *'registered social landlords'* where tenants agreed. This went far beyond anything that previous Conservative administrations had thought politically possible but actually chimed with Tony Blair's view of local government as a *'flawed model'* for the provision of services where *'the council was – and often still is – an unresponsive and incompetent landlord'* (quoted, and challenged by, Malpass, 2005, p194). The aim was the physical improvement of council and housing association stock to the Decent Homes Standard apparently at minimal cost to the *public* purse. In order to ensure this, overseen by Nick Raynsford as Housing Minister (one of nine in New Labour's thirteen years in power), the Department of the Environment, Transport and the Regions (p61) would,

> *'From 2001-2002 ... support the transfer of up to 200,000 dwellings each year. If local authorities submit transfer proposals at that level, and if tenants support them, registered social landlords will become the majority providers of social housing from 2004 onwards.'*

The backlog of council repairs and modernisation (estimated at £19billion by DETR) had been an acute concern for local authority councillors and staff for many years, but they had not expected this. The approach received minimal support in the responses to the Green Paper and consequently, in reality, was controversial. Authorities had to undertake an 'option appraisal' to decide the best route to attain the Decent Homes Standard by 2010. The Standard was a carrot-like inducement to many tenants to support transfer. For local authorities it was more problematic. Most Labour authorities, especially the large metropolitan authorities, delayed until mid-decade and the invention of the arm's length management organisation (ALMO). They knew they were faced with a true Hobson's Choice of variations of privatisation: whole or partial stock transfer, housing private finance initiative or the ALMO (if one accepts an ALMO as a mid-way stalking horse). Attaining the Decent Homes Standard was often only possible by using these alternatives. Extra funds would be realised via these routes whilst, if tenants voted to stay with their council landlord, there was no extra funding for modernisation and major repair work.

Nearly one million properties have been transferred to housing associations or housing companies since 1997 (and 1.4 million since 1988) but this policy has been exceptionally controversial. It is remarkable that New Labour have chosen to continue with it with such tenacity. The considerable challenges to this approach should have given any socialist party pause for thought and opportunity for a 'u-turn.' Aside from the costs, the main issues for socialists have been the lack of democratic accountability in stock transfer associations and housing companies, concerns about the long-term purpose of ALMOs, and the lack of a 'level playing field' between these organisations and local authority landlords in attaining the Decent Homes Standard. For example, Gibb and Whitehead (2007, p193) remarked that *'more than £6 billion of private funded investment has gone directly into improving transferred housing'* and then, citing Wilcox (2003, table 68a), they added,

> *'The evidence on English council transfers suggests that there has been considerable refinancing based on equity growth in the former council stock. For the 120 council transfers that took place in England between 1988-89 and 2002-3 (nearly three quarters of a million dwellings in total), the total (cash) loan facility generated was £11.181 billion, of which only £5.503 billion was accounted for by the cash terms transfer price of the cumulative transferred stock, and within that figure only just over £3 billion was council housing debt.'*

In other words, stock transfer associations in that period used the benefit of former council assets to generate substantial additional funds, to pay for additional maintenance and modernisation (perhaps Decent Homes Plus) and other capital expenditure (for example, new offices). This was possible because the property was likely to be in better condition, had been positively valued on transfer from the local authority and property prices generally were rising at this time. So it was seen as a good investment by banks and building societies. It is no surprise that tenants and staff have been positive about their new landlords' improvements (Pawson and Fancy, 2003). But there is an alternative view of these financial arrangements. They provide an example of the private sector (associations and housing companies) benefiting from what had (until recently) been public sector assets. Additionally, new debt had been loaded on to the transferred housing to be paid for by tenants through rents/housing benefit and Right to Buy sales.

The financial costs of implementing this programme of different forms of privatisation have been considerable, especially in relation to the transaction costs associated with large scale voluntary stock transfers. This includes the cost of consultants, legal fees and the expense of running the ballot required: £424.3million for 160 positively valued transfers from 1988 to 2008 and £41.7million for 52 negatively valued transfers in the period 2002 to 2008 (Wilcox, 2008, p168 and p171). In order to 'encourage' northern authorities with poor quality stock, partial transfers became possible and debt write off and/or 'gap' funding of £5 billion was made available by government to deal with any differences between the sale price to a new organisation and the level of debt the local authority still held at the time of transfer (Pawson, 2009, p29). Then the Arms Length Management Organisation (ALMO) was invented: in many ways a local authority managing agent but in others a possible route to privatisation. Additional government funds have been available for ALMOs through a programme of six bidding rounds. For the most recent three year period, running from 2008/9 to 2010/11, £2.4 billion was available from government to support the most high performing organisations in their work to reach the Decent Homes Standard. Finally, the most expensive and complicated option is the housing Private Finance Initiative (PFI). The Government originally set aside £2.7 billion to support these private sector consortia but it has spent much more than that on the 29 council housing PFIs in existence. They have recently been criticized for cost overruns: since 1998, 21 of the 25 projects actually signed have experienced *'cost increases ... 12 of which were over 100%'* and *'value for money'* could not be demonstrated (National Audit Office, 2010, p7).

Up until 2007, the government largely ignored persistent and determined campaigning by tenants trying to find a way in which councils could retain the management and improvement of their stock directly (the so-called 'Fourth Option'). The challenge to the New Labour leadership exhibited through conference resolutions at the annual Party Conference supporting the 'Fourth Option' was dealt with by rule changes to prevent resolutions being put at all! The work of the House of Commons Council Housing Group (House of Commons Council Housing Group, 2006 and 2010) was not accepted by the New Labour leadership, though supported by increasing numbers of backbench MPs.

However, with a change of Prime Minister, and following a new Green Paper, *Homes for the future: more affordable, more sustainable* (CLG, 2007), there were signs that this might change. Although housing associations were again given the major role, local authorities might be allowed to build again on a small scale. The credit crunch put extra pressure on the government as house-building targets, announced with the Green Paper, began to look increasingly unattainable. Was this Harloe's 'strategic moment' arriving now that owner-occupation and the banking industry had spectacularly imploded again? Indeed, a larger programme of council housebuilding was agreed. The 'fourth option' of council housebuilding and major renovation looked even more possible in the future following consultation relating to proposed changes in local authority Housing Revenue Accounts which would enable local authorities to become self-financing (CLG, 2009). Millions needed secure, cheap, good quality rented housing.

In the context of the recession, would council housing (or 'social housing' more generally) now be seen as an attractive option?

'Mixed communities' or 'ghettos of deprivation'?

This brings us finally to consider housing management. We will focus on standards, the fragmentation and lack of democratic accountability in associations and housing companies, the implications of New Labour's version of *'mixed communities'* and the impact on *'social housing'* of policy developed by the Home Office to deal with *'anti-social behaviour.'*

Standards

Margaret Thatcher had little time for local authority landlordism, preferring housing associations and private landlords, even though there was scant evidence to justify such a preference (DoE, 1989; Bines, Kemp, Pleace and Radley, 1993). Tony Blair was also antagonistic towards local authority direct service provision. Each introduced a regulatory system supposedly to improve standards (compulsory competitive tendering and best value respectively) but based on private sector market measures of quality. Excessive regulation and the recent focus on efficiency savings experienced by local authorities and housing associations (or *'registered providers'* as they are now described) not surprisingly have diminished cultures of public service replacing them with managerialism and pseudo-consumerism (see the discussion in Jordan, 2008, pp232-44 about the limitations of the economic model and contract approach to public policy).

Fragmentation and democratic accountability

Housing management has always been weakly professionalised but now it is also excessively fragmented due to the stock transfer strategies of New Labour (with local authorities, associations, housing companies, tenant management organisations, co-operatives, ALMOs and PFI consortia all potentially managing stock within a local authority's boundaries). Although local authorities now have a strategic role, this has developed in a piecemeal fashion. Social housing organisations are often unco-ordinated locally except in partnerships of various kinds and quality. Yet some associations and companies are connected in unexpected ways, not perceptible by the public (or tenants) via mergers and group structures. For example, forty percent of stock transfer associations have become part of group structures (Pawson and Sosenko, 2008). Other associations or ALMOs engage in (re)branding exercises which effectively disguise their history and character. This is the *'quasi-market'* (le Grand and Bartlett, 1993) of *'social housing'* in which *'registered providers'* now operate. Margaret Thatcher wanted to create this market, through the breakup of what the Conservatives saw as monopolies of local authority housing (at the same time undermining what they believed were Labour-voting strongholds). New Labour has actually done it: most whole or partial stock transfers have taken place since 1997.

Less accountable, highly complex organisational forms, concentrating solely on the concerns of *'the businesss,'* have grown in the vacuums created by local authority transfers. Recruitment to association 'Boards' via individual shareholding is reliant variously on individuals coming forward due to personal interest, the social and professional contacts of existing Board members or the organisation publically advertising for particular expertise or Board positions. Housing companies (set up to receive large scale stock transfers) and ALMOs have a slightly different Board structure, where one third of Board members may be local authority councillors nominated by the local authority to serve for three years. However, they are usually backbench councillors – a democratic deficit resulting from Tony Blair's modernisation of local government. Another democratic deficit is evident in that the sector's fragmentation has left stock transfer organisations and ALMO tenants and applicants with less direct representation (through elected councillors) and created a situation in which Chief Officers/Chief Executives are less accountable to stock transfer Boards than they were to 'old style' local authority Housing Committees or 'new style' Cabinets. Is this the *'empowerment'* that New Labour promised in its 1997 election manifesto and 2000 Green Paper *'Quality and Choice'*?

'Mixed' communities

As will have been clear from earlier parts of this discussion, socialists from previous generations believed *'mass'* council housing was a positive force especially when built on a large-scale. Building in this way, local authorities (especially Labour controlled authorities) managed to provide good quality housing that has been valued by millions of tenants (ironically nearly two million have bought their home as a consequence). Labour authorities also built to break the link between poverty and poor housing that was common for working-class households before the Second World War. Council housing has varied in quality and durability over different decades: much was in poor condition by the time of the

General Election in 1997 due to years of disinvestment by former Labour and Conservative administrations. But never before has a government so determinedly sought to dismantle the sector and change the people who live in particular areas, especially if they lived in areas considered to be *'ghettos of deprivation'* (DETR, 2000). New Labour wanted *'mixed'* communities in existing estates where possible and 'mixed' tenure in any newly built housing developments. The Green Paper stated clearly (p37) that their objective was to,

> *'... promote a better mix of housing tenures, creating stable, mixed-income communities rather than ghettos of poor and vulnerable people.'*

Why was this? Some thought it was to protect investment; others that *'concentrated'* poverty has independent effects, and that council (or housing association) tenants might be disadvantaged simply by living in the sector (see Gregory, 2009, pp31-45). This idea needed to be strongly challenged, not just through argument (Ellery, 2008; Fletcher, Gore, Reeve and Robertson, 2008) but also through action. New Labour could have built on a large scale and enabled local authorities again to create the 'living tapestries' of communities that Bevan is remembered for. Inclusive allocations policies based on housing need could have ensured the rehousing into secure, good quality council homes of citizens who are poor through being reliant on state benefits and/or low waged 'flexible' work. Instead, policy turned inwards and focused on poor council and housing association tenants and applicants. The emphasis became breaking up *'concentrations'* of the poor who were already tenants (through allocations and transfer policies) and cajoling the unemployed poor (applicants and tenants) to take paid work (following Hills, 2008) and, at one point, planning to restrict offers of housing only to those who were in paid work or actively seeking it (Ellery, 2008).

More generally, social landlords were expected to adopt a choice based lettings (CBL) scheme by 2010 for the majority of vacancies in existing stock (DETR, 2000). This was intended to encourage a wider range of people to consider social housing but in a system where *'demand'* is high, it is questionable whether there has been much genuine choice. Instead, the change from allocations based on *'housing need'* to lettings based on *'choice'* has had detrimental effects (to varying degrees) on people who are vulnerable, old or homeless. Those who are most vulnerable are least likely to understand the choice based lettings *'bidding'* process and, unless helped to bid, will lose out to better informed and skilled applicants. Since 2004, the government also has put pressure on local authorities to reduce the numbers of statutory homeless accepted for rehousing through 'homeless *prevention*' work. Laudable in some respects, the route to assessment under the homeless legislation may be obscured by 'prevention' work with housing staff trying to find alternatives to a formal homeless assessment, possibly in the less secure private rented sector (Office of the Deputy Prime Minister, 2005a; Pawson, 2007). Local authorities and housing associations also have been encouraged to consider local lettings schemes for particular areas where the *'social profile'* needs to change. New Labour has even justified the Right to Buy in this light (DETR, 2000, p37) claiming,

> 'In many cases, it has encouraged more affluent tenants to remain in the neighbourhoods they have lived in for many years, helping to create stable, mixed-income communities.'

Most new rented 'social housing' has been provided by associations since 1997 through combinations of private borrowing, public grant and financial surpluses generated internally from property sales. New rented housing has also been provided by private developers who have to provide a handful of rented homes on private estates to obtain local authority planning permission (nationally, an average of 40% of social rented housing is obtained in this way). Generally, new social rented properties are 'pepper-potted' within predominantly private estates, dominated by mortgaged owner-occupiers (who may now be finding their financial situation increasingly precarious). Managing this stock is more expensive for the landlord and from the tenants' point of view, undermines any collective sense of sharing a landlord, making it more difficult to campaign to obtain improvements. 'Mixing' tenure like this in new predominantly private estates has become a proxy for mixing income but poor and vulnerable people are being 'mixed' very thinly – a very pale, twenty-first century version of the communities that Bevan had in mind sixty years ago.

Underlying this is the belief that poor residents in social housing will gain by having wealthier neighbours in owner-occupied homes who might act as role models and provide work contacts to strengthen tenants' *'bridging social capital,'* helping them into the world of paid work. The few studies that have examined residents' contacts in *'mixed'* neighbourhoods question whether outward-facing personal contacts are constructed and used like this (Allen, Camina, Casey,

Coward, and Wood, 2005; Silverman, Lupton and Fenton, 2005). *'Bridging social capital'* appears a long way from Bevan's idea of a *'living tapestry'* of a community: instead personal relationships are measured instrumentally and, most importantly, oriented to securing and keeping paid work.

The example of Park Hill in Sheffield (see pages 26-27) suggests some of the possible difficulties (though there are many other examples across the country). Over one thousand former council tenants and their families have been rehoused out of Park Hill via the local authority since 2003. Only fifty-six households will return. Where will the rented flats be located in the new Park Hill? Will they be indistinguishable from those that are bought? How will low income and possibly vulnerable residents mix with wealthy owner occupiers who are seeking a *'fashionable'* address and lively lifestyle?

We would argue that using *'mixed'* tenure as a proxy for genuine mixing of household types, range of incomes and variety of interests and involvements is flawed. New Labour's view of 'mixed communities' has been used more as a smokescreen to hide the serious decline in council and housing association building for rent. What is really needed is what Jordan has described more generally as,

> '... a new version of collective life, made up of networks, movements and relationships [including] institutions through which people collectively deliberate and interpret their experiences and try to improve the quality of their lives, outside of the pressure to produce, deliver and consume.'
>
> (Jordan, 2008, p249)

'Anti-social behaviour'

Tony Blair's negative view of council housing and local authorities has provided the motor for stock transfer, but this has been played out in other policy interventions relating to the sector. The most obvious instance is that of crime and policing.

This paper has described how, in more positive times, allocations policies enhanced the possibility of a wide range of households living in council housing. Whilst there have always been families that have had multiple problems, in general, handling 'nuisance' has been proportionate: one element in a much wider housing management remit. But more recently Crawford (2009, p219) has referred to Office of the Deputy Prime Minister policy documents which linked housing policy and *'community safety'* (ODPM, 2005b). And successive comments from Home Office Ministers (along with the high profile interventions of a small number of authorities) have created a situation in which *'anti-social behaviour'* (ASB) is inextricably linked to social housing, especially council housing. Was it acceptable that Home Office Ministers referred to young people as *'feral'*, *'yobs'* and *'louts'* (targeting them with anti social behaviour orders) and made persistent comments about *'neighbours from hell'*, echoing Frank Field's worst interventions (Parr and Nixon, 2009, p103)?

A veritable torrent of legislation has been enacted since 1997 to deal with *'anti-social behaviour.'* Some is draconian (with restrictions on movement and association, reduced requirements for evidence before criminal conviction and public shaming). This has undermined the Labour Party's reputation in relation to civil liberties. Much has been targeted against council and housing association tenants, particularly young people who live on estates (where *'bad'* parenting and anti-

---

Park Hill, Sheffield – a new mixed community?

The Park Hill estate occupies a prime position just outside the city centre and provides a striking backdrop to city centre regeneration pro-jects. It is a gateway to Sheffield. In 2003, in con-junction with English Partnerships (the national regeneration agency), the City Council began to put together a vision for the future of the estate, which was to [enable the] mixed tenure, mixed use transformation of Park Hill as a fashionable City centre address.

[This would be made up of]
- 257 flats for sale
- 56 flats for rent
- 12 flats for shared ownership
- A new GPs surgery and nursery
- Retail and leisure facilities
- High quality public realm

History Park Hill was the first completed post-war slum clearance scheme of an entire community in Britain. It was the most ambitious inner-city development of its time. In 1954 work began on the design of Park Hill and it was later built between 1957 and 1961. Within the old Park area architects recognised there was a strong sense of local community and, in the design of Park Hill, tried to

social behaviour apparently now go hand-in-hand). Social landlords have been expected to police much of it especially in relation to anti-social behaviour orders and acceptable behaviour contracts. However, there have been real differences between New Labour's policy concerns and staff working with people labelled in this way. Parr and Nixon (2009, p108), referring to staff involved in dealing with '*anti-social behaviour*' and family intervention project work, pointed out that on an individual basis,

> '... rather than construct the "anti-social" pathologically as morally deficient or wilfully irresponsible ... [there were] alternative interpretations of the "problem" of ASB, with a greater focus on the multi-faceted nature of the underlying causes.'

More broadly, Crawford (2009) has referred to '*governing through crime*' now being a '*major component of modern social housing*' (p220)

---

preserve this community spirit. Where possible, neighbours were rehoused alongside each other in the new complex and each flat opens out onto a 10 foot wide deck. This provided access for milk floats and communal areas, enhancing the image of 'streets in the sky'.

The Estate The building alone covers an area of 17 acres and currently contains around 1,000 flats. In total the whole site covers 32 acres. The slope of the site inspired the idea of a continuous roof line which results in the height of the blocks varying dramatically from 4 storeys at the top of the estate, rising to 13 storeys towards the City centre. Over the years the estate has been home to 31 shops, 4 pubs, 74 garages, a primary and a nursery school, doctor's surgery and pharmacy. The shops were set at the lowest point of the estate, to which people were thought to naturally gravitate. 4 pubs and a laundrette were more widely dispersed at points on the ground near lifts.

Surveys commissioned [in 2003] showed the need for a reduction in Council rented units on the estate. The partners proposed a split in the number of units to 1/3 social rented, 1/3 market sale and 1/3 commercial space. In April 2004, an advert was placed to select a Registered Social Landlord and Developer partner. Parkway Housing (Manchester Methodist Housing Group) and Urban Splash were selected. Most of the funding will come from Urban Splash as the Developer. However, the public sector will contribute - Transform South Yorkshire, the Government's Housing Market Renewal Agency (£13m), the Homes and Communities Agency (£14m for gap funding, £10m to provide 200 units for rent and 40 units for shared ownership), Parkway Housing (£10m contribution towards this) and English Heritage (£0.5m for specialist concrete repairs).

Source: Sheffield City Council's website 2010

especially in relation to checking and controlling the behaviour of tenants and visitors. But again, it remains the case that different social landlords differ in what they do. The resources available vary locally as does the effectiveness of local *community safety* partnerships. Landlords also differ in their awareness of differences and antagonisms in local areas and the possibility that these may fuel complaints as much as actual problems, especially when considering young people. (Crawford provided detail relating to New Earswick, in York, where older residents had difficulty coming to terms with younger residents. They expressed this in the form of demands for extra local policing which the landlord initially paid for.)

Policy nationally changed in emphasis when Gordon Brown became Prime Minister in 2007, moving from discipline to *'support'* through the Respect programme (established nationally in 2006). But the issue was always vulnerable to politicians' populist tendencies. For example, Gordon Brown's renewed emphasis on using ASBOs as punishment after the Labour Party Conference in 2009 was possibly anticipating general election campaign issues.

The largely negative emphasis of the policy in relation to anti-social-behaviour, and the way it has developed and been publicised, has seriously affected social housing, especially council housing. We would argue that it has changed the way the sector is viewed by the general public. Council tenants in 1997 were stigmatized as *'poor'* and *'dependent'* but there was some hope that New Labour might improve that perception. By 2010, council (and housing association) tenants were now more likely to be viewed as *'poor'*, *'dependent'* and riddled with *'anti-social behaviour.'* This is akin to attitudes towards tenants in public housing in America, living in a sector which is widely believed to reinforce *'dependency'*, restrict *'mobility'* and generate *'crime'* (Ireland, Thornberry and Loeber, 2009). This is now part of New Labour's legacy.

New Labour's legacy

Thirteen years ago New Labour was elected on a manifesto promise that it would be both *'radical'* and *'modern'*. We have argued that, released from the responsibilities of what it chose to call *'outdated* [socialist] *ideology,* the party maintained the Conservative direction of travel established by Margaret Thatcher and John Major in relation to council housing and *social housing* more generally. Worse still, New Labour has gone much further than perhaps Thatcher and Major would have dared. In doing so, it has collectively failed to protect the poorest and most vulnerable and has done little to provide collectively for the well being and security of anyone who either does not want or cannot afford to buy a home. They have created a situation in which the future under a Conservative/Liberal alliance is looking increasingly dismal for anyone on a *social housing* waiting or transfer list or for council and ALMO tenants hoping for a secure future.

If New Labour had abolished the Right to Buy and instituted a large scale local authority building and modernisation programme, if it had created a sector of good quality affordable rented housing that a wide range of citizens might be proud to live in and that was democratically accountable, we would now be looking at a completely different scenario. As it is, they failed collectively to recognize the once-in-a-lifetime opportunity presented to them by their election in 1997. In doing so, thirteen years of New Labour have made it much easier for the Conservatives and Liberals to cut and transfer and abolish. Welcome to the twenty-first century *'modern'* welfare state.

Postscript

David Cameron, the new Prime Minister, in a 'question and answer' session in Birmingham in August 2010, announced that the government has plans to scrap secure tenancies for council tenants (and housing association tenants who have them). This announcement is in direct contradiction of promises he made publically just before the general election that the Conservatives had no such intentions.

He now has said that new tenants will be given a fixed term tenancy of between five and ten years' length which will be subject to regular review. If a tenant's household circumstances improve, they will be forced to move out. If the tenant dies, no-one will be allowed to succeed to the tenancy if they have been living as a member of the household, as they can now: they will be forced to move out. If they find over time they *'under-occupy'* their homes (for example, pensioner households with grown up children who have moved out), they could be forced to accept smaller housing, whether or not they want to move.

Cameron claims this will create a *'flexible'* system, promoting social mobility whilst at the same time making best use of a scarce resource. He has said that there will be consultation on these changes and that they will be included in the Decentralisation and Localism Bill to be considered by parliament later in 2010.

Glossary

ALMO – An arm's length management organisation established by a local authority to manage its housing stock and improve it to the Decent Homes Standard by 2010/2012. Usually having a five year life, extra funding was available to ALMOs to manage and refurbish the stock to the Standard.

Decent Homes Standard (DHS) and Decent Homes Plus – To meet the Standard, the property has to meet the statutory minimum fitness standard or, from 2006, the Housing Health and Safety Rating standard, be in a reasonable state of repair, have reasonably modern facilities and services, and provide a reasonable amount of thermal comfort. Decent Homes Plus is simply a higher level of modernization. The expectation is that 92% of social housing (council and housing association owned) will reach the DHS by the end of 2010. A report by the House of Commons Public Accounts Committee estimated that 305,000 social sector homes will still be non-decent at December 2010.

Dudley Committee – Its report was published in 1944 and its main recommendations included in the Housing Manual available to local authorities. It focused on the lack of variety in pre-Second World War council house building, the amount of space available (including storage) and improvements to the fittings to be included in kitchens and bathrooms.

Housing Revenue Account – The HRA records all income in relation to the provision of a council housing management service. It is ring-fenced and controlled by central government subsidy arrangements and other restrictions.

Housing Investment Programme – The HIP was an annual allocation of capital expenditure to individual local authorities. It could include such items as the costs of buying and building on land, housing repairs if money had to be borrowed and other capital grants associated with building/refurbishment. The HIP programme was discontinued in 1990.

Housing Association Grant (HAG) – This was a grant made by the Housing Corporation to associations to enable them to build or improve property for letting. Before the 1988 Housing Act, the grant covered nearly all development costs. After 1988, it was only available in fixed amounts (fixed HAG) which varied by property type and location and reduced each year. It was renamed and currently exists as Social Housing Grant (SHG).

Housing Corporation – A government quango which oversaw the activities of registered social landlords. It allocated capital funding and supervised the activities of associations more generally. It was abolished in November 2008 and its functions were split between the Homes and Communities Agency and the Tenant Services Authority.

Private Finance Initiative(PFI) – A complex funding mechanism through which consortia of private firms contract with a local authority to improve and manage typically single estates for periods of 25 to 30 years, taking on the risks of improvement in exchange for a management fee. Housing PFIs are relatively rare in social housing because of the complexities of the process.

References

Allen, C., Camina, M., Casey, R., Coward, S. and Wood, M. (2005) *Mixed tenure twenty years on: nothing out of the ordinary*, Coventry: Chartered Institute of Housing with the Joseph Rowntree Foundation

Bines, W., Kemp, P., Pleace, N. and Radley, C. (1993) *Managing social housing*, London: HMSO

Blunkett, D. and Green, G. (1983) *Building from the bottom: the Sheffield experience*, London: Fabian Society

Bowley, M. (1945) *Housing and the state 1919-1944*, London: Allen and Unwin

Burnett, J. (1986 second edition) *A social history of housing 1815-1985*, London: Methuen

Burrows, R. (2003) *Home-ownership and poverty in Britain*, JRF Findings, http://www.jrf.or.uk/sites/files/jrf/113.pdf accessed 30 July 2009

Campbell, J. (2003) *Margaret Thatcher, Volume Two: The Iron Lady*, London: Jonathan Cape

Communities and Local Government (2007) *Valuing for Right to Buy*, available on http://www.communities.gov.uk/archived/publications/housing/valuingright?view=Standard accessed on 7 July 2010

Communities and Local Government (2007) *Homes for the future: more affordable, more sustainable*, London: The Stationery Office, Cm 7191

Communities and Local Government (2009) *Reform of council housing finance: Consultation*, London: The Stationery Office

Crawford, A. (2009) 'Policing and community safety in residential areas: the mixed economy of visible patrols' in Flint, J. (ed) *Housing, urban governance and anti-social behaviour*, Bristol: Policy Press, pp219-38

Daunton, M.J. (1984) *Councillors and tenants: local authority housing in English cities 19919-1939*, Leicester: Leicester University Press

Department of the Environment (1987) *Housing: the Government's Proposals*, London: HMSO, Cmd 214

Department of the Environment (1989) *The nature and effectiveness of housing management in England, A report to the Department of the Environment by the Centre for Housing Research University of Glasgow*, London: HMSO

Department of the Environment, Transport and the Regions/Department of Social Security (2000) *Quality and Choice : A Decent Home for All*, London: The Stationery Office

Ellery, S. (2008) 'Report blows Flint's work-to-live ideas out of the water' in *Inside Housing*, 21 August 2008

Fletcher, D,R., Gore, T., Reeve, K. and Robinson, D. (2008) *Social housing and worklessness: key policy messages, Research report No 482*, London: Department for Work and Pensions

Foot, M. (1997) *Aneurin Bevan 1897-1960*, London: Victor Gollancz

Forrest, R. and Murie, A. (1991 second edition) *Selling the welfare state: the privatisation of public housing*, London: Routledge

Housing: Did it have to be like this?

Gibb, K. and Whitehead, C. (2007) 'Towards the more effective use of housing finance and subsidy' in *Housing Studies*, volume 22, number 2, pp183-200

Gregory, J. (2009) *In the mix: narrowing the gap between public and private housing*, Fabian Policy Report 62, London: Fabian Society

Hannan, J., (1988), *The life of John Wheatley*, Nottingham: Spokesman

Harloe, M. (1995) *The people's home? Social rented housing in Europe and America*, Oxford: Blackwell

Hills, J. (2007) *Ends and means: the future roles of social housing in England, CASE report 34*, ESRC Research Centre for Analysis of Social Exclusion: London School of Economics

House of Commons Council Housing Group (2006) *Support for the 'fourth option for council housing'* available at www.support4councilhousing.org.uk/report/resources/HOCCHG_report.pdf

House of Commons Council Housing Group (2010) *Council housing: time to invest: fair funding, investment and building council housing. Our report to the Government's Review of Council Housing Finance*, available at www.support4councilhousing.org.uk/report/resources/HOCCHG_TimeToInvest.pdf accessed 6 July 2010

Inside Housing (2010) 'Labour's legacy' 7th May 2010 http://www.insidehousing.co.uk/analysis/in-depth/labour's-legacy/6509704.article accessed 6 July 2010

Ireland, T.O., Thornberry, T.P. and Loeber, R. (2009) 'Residential stability among adolescents in public housing: a risk factor for delinquent and violent behaviour?' in Flint, J. (ed) *Housing, urban governance and anti-social behaviour*, Bristol: Policy Press, pp301-24

Jacobs, K. (1999) *The dynamics of local housing policy: a study of council housing renewal in the London Borough of Hackney*, Aldershot: Ashgate

Jordan. B. (2008) *Welfare and well being: social value in public policy*, Bristol: Policy Press

Le Grand, J. and Bartlett, W. (eds) (1993) *Quasi-markets and social policy*, Basingstoke: Macmillan

Malpass, P. (2005) *Housing and the welfare state*, Basingstoke: Palgrave Macmillan

Malpass, P. (2008) 'Housing and the new welfare state' in *Housing Studies*, volume 23, number 1, pp1-19

Malpass, P. and Murie, A. (1990 third edition) *Housing policy and practice*, London: Macmillan

Merrett, S. (1979) *State housing in Britain*, London: Routledge & Kegan Paul

Miliband, R. (1972 second edition) *Parliamentary socialism – a study in the politics of Labour*, London: Merlin Press

National Audit Office (2010) *PFI in housing*, Report by the Comptroller and Auditor General, HC 71, Session 2010-1011, London: The Stationery Office

ODPM (2005a) *Providing more settled homes*, London: ODPM